Finding My Way to Grace

A 14-day Devotional Journey to Deliverance

JUSTIN ROSS-HILLARD

FINDING MY WAY TO GRACE
A 14-DAY DEVOTIONAL JOURNEY TO DELIVERANCE
Copyright © 2015 by Justin Ross-Hillard
All rights reserved.

Published by:
NyreePress Literary Group
P.O. Box 164882
Fort Worth, TX 76161
www.nyreepress.com

Cover design by:
Graphic Design by S. Michelle
http://sherilynbennett.crevado.com/

Scripture taken from the Holy Bible, NEW INTERNATIONAL VERSION®, NIV® Copyright © 1973, 1978, 1984, 2011 by Biblica, Inc.® Used by permission. All rights reserved worldwide.
NEW INTERNATIONAL VERSION® and NIV® are registered trademarks of Biblica, Inc. Use of either trademark for the offering of goods or services requires the prior written consent of Biblica US, Inc.

All rights reserved. No part of this book may be used or reproduced by any means, graphic, electronic, or mechanical, including photocopying, recording, taping or by any information storage retrieval system without the written permission of the publisher. Copying this book is both illegal and unethical.

ISBN print: 978-0-9860866-2-5

Library of Congress Control Number: 2015933888
Christian Living / Devotional / Prayer

Printed in the United States of America

Dedication

To all who dream and invest in those dreams. Even when you've given your all, continue to dream and invest.

To my mother, Marie, to whom I owe my passion for reading and writing, you set me up for this and I thank you.

To my wife, Amaris, for supporting and believing in me and pushing me to make it happen. This is just the beginning.

To my children, Justin and Payton: the ministry of Grace is your spiritual legacy. I want you to grow up always knowing that you are loved and accepted. Always continue to strive to be the best God has purposed you to be.

Finding My Way to Grace

A 14-day Devotional Journey to Deliverance

NYREEPRESS
Dallas / Fort-Worth, Texas

Table of Contents

DAY ONE:	Why embark on this journey?	10
DAY TWO:	God wants who?	14
DAY THREE:	Understanding your starting point.	18
DAY FOUR:	I fight, I fall, I fight again.	22
DAY FIVE:	It's in my mind.	26
DAY SIX:	Why do I need this? (the past)	30
DAY SEVEN:	Why I need this. (the present)	34
DAY EIGHT:	Why I need this. (the future)	38
DAY NINE:	My hunger exceeds my reach.	42
DAY TEN:	Grace: A gift others need.	46
DAY ELEVEN:	Grace: A gift I need.	50
DAY TWELVE:	Freedom ain't free.	54
DAY THIRTEEN:	Setting continuous goals.	58
DAY FOURTEEN:	I'm moving forward, but I'm still me	62

"When I opened my eyes to *Grace*, I saw the world as *Jesus* sees it – a beautiful creation in process to becoming better."

— *Justin Ross-Hillard*

Introduction

I have been a part of the Church for as long as I can remember. I have loved God, His people and what happens when we all get together. However, I haven't always known the Grace of God. We hear it in Church all the time- many have written big books about it. Yet, finding the real meaning of Grace is difficult for many and recognizing how it factors into life can be equally challenging.

That leads me into why I wrote this book. There was a time in my life that I didn't know the real impact Grace was making on, and more importantly, in me. When I opened my eyes to Grace, I saw the world as Jesus sees it – a beautiful creation in process to becoming better. In a world filled with chaos, at the end of the day, it has always been God's desire to be in direct relationship with us and by relationship help us become better. This is why God sent His only begotten son on our behalf. Grace is a constant reminder of the extent of God's love and His big idea for our lives.

As you read this book, it is written in devotional format for you to use as a guide for fourteen consecutive days. That doesn't mean that you can't spend more than one day on a subject- do what feels right- but enjoy this journey. Allow God to tell you when it's time to turn the page. For the rest of your life you will be in process: something in your life will always be in development. The Grace life is a process and while it's freely given by God without measure, the extent of how much you receive depends on how aware you are of its presence. Use each day and topic to open your eyes and ears to the great work God is doing in your life.

Finally, it's important to me that I remind you that being in the "process" is sometimes not easy and uncomfortable. As you journey through this book it will become uneasy at times but don't stop. Confront the difficult moments head on knowing that Grace is with you and on your side.

I found my way to Grace and I know you will too.

Day One:

Why embark on this journey?

*H*ave you ever awakened from sleep knowing what you need to get done but not having the energy to do it? We all have had a day like that. Becoming better at being you is no different. Most of the time, we are keenly aware of what we need to do to become our best self.

"I need to lost weight."
"I need to eat right."
"I need to go back to school."
"I need to find better friends."

You know what needs to be done. The question is, do you have the energy to do it? Many times you'll find that it takes someone else getting in your face and pointing out your issues before you take the steps necessary to do what needs to be done and the last thing you, me or anyone else need's is someone else giving us an opinion about what we should be doing; but that's the problem. We know, but we won't do. The reason you picked up this book is because you are ready to do all the things you've been waiting on. We are preparing to go on a journey that will bring us closer to ourselves and smack dab into the desires God has for us.

Don't question the how or the when. Let's just start walking and see what happens. Why this journey? Because you need to do it. You want to do it. This is the moment you've been longing for.

Jeremiah 29:11-13: "'For I know the thoughts that I think toward you,' says the Lord, 'thoughts of peace and not of evil, to give you a future and a hope. Then you will call upon Me and go and pray to Me, and I will listen to you. And you will seek Me and find Me, when you search for Me with all your heart.'"

Prayer:

Father, thank you that you have led me to this place. I am open to walk with you. Help me not to walk ahead or drag my feet behind you. I am learning to trust you on this new journey. In Jesus' name, AMEN.

Name three things you know you need to do to become your best self.

1. _____

2. _____

3. _____

Day Two:

God wants who?

One of the most difficult things to get people to understand is that God wants YOU. God created you, chose you, stood right beside you from the time you were conceived to this very moment. There is nothing about you—where you've been or what you've done—that is hidden from God. Unlike your family and friends, you get to be 100% your real self when you spend time with God.

The first step on this journey to discovering grace is to accept that **God wants you**. Imperfect, moody, cussing, nasty, and indecisive. Yes, God wants you. Not because God wants to change you, but because God wants you to know that nothing you've done or could do can take the love of God away from you. Noah was a drunk and was saved from the flood, Moses a murderer and he led God's people from Egypt, David was an adulterer and God chose him to be King. Grace is God's purposeful and willful action of stepping into the impossibilities of our lives and defying the structure of the rules so much that what once was not, now is. Prior to this moment, you might have thought God didn't want you, but now you know: God has always wanted you.

Romans 8:37-39: "Yet in all these things we are more than conquerors through Him who loved us. For I am persuaded that neither death nor life, nor angels nor principalities nor powers, nor things present nor things to come, nor height nor depth, nor any other created thing, shall be able to separate us from the love of God which is in Christ Jesus our Lord."

Prayer:

My loving Father, I need you to forgive me for not trusting your choice. You choosing me was not an accident. I ask for wisdom as I keep walking this journey knowing you're here because you want to be with me. Thank you, Lord! In Jesus' name, Amen.

1. Write 3 things you've done that you think would make God leave you?

    1. _____
    2. _____
    3. _____

2. Name three times in your life when you know God was near you.

    1. _____
    2. _____
    3. _____

Day Three:

Understanding your starting point.

*E*verybody has a history. HIS-tory and HER-story; this is your starting point. What is the story written on the pages of your life's book? Are you willing to share with others the codex of your life? History almost always plagues and impedes our progress when we deem our experiences bad or negative. We hold ourselves back because we're focused on what we didn't do or what we should have said. The past is behind you.

If you don't make the decision to move forward from your starting point, you will simply stay there. In Genesis chapters 38-50, we find the story of a young man named Joseph whom God chose to bless. Joseph went through a lot for this blessing. He was hated by his brothers, thrown in a pit, sold into slavery, lied on, thrown in prison on false rape charges, and forgotten. Yet, in the midst of his starting point, he never let his past beat him down. He kept moving. At the end of the most difficult part of Joseph's story, he made sense of everything that happened in his life.

"But Joseph said to them, "Don't be afraid. Am I in the place of God? You intended to harm me, but God intended it for good to accomplish what is now being done, the saving of many lives," (Genesis 50:19-20).

Joseph's reflection to his brothers was that even though they meant to hurt him, God used it all to save many lives. On this journey, every part of your life matters and will be used by God to touch others even when you do not see the end result.

Romans 8:28: "And we know, all things are working together for the good of them who are the Called according to His purpose."

Prayer:

Lord, sometimes I think too much about the past. I need you to help me not live in the past but to know that my past is taking part in my future victory. I receive grace to know that you will use everything about me for your glory. Amen.

Questions:

1. Name two milestone events (good and bad) that have shaped your life?

    1. _____
    2. _____

2. Describe one hurtful moment in your life that is painful to talk about with others.

    _____
    _____
    _____

Day Four:

I fight, I fall, I fight again.

Muhammad Ali once said, "I hated every minute of training, but I said, 'Don't quit. Suffer now and live the rest of your life as a champion.'" This life filled with Grace we are developing takes time, but you have to realize that you're in training. Training hurts. Training smells bad. After training, the next day you will get up hurting more than when you went to bed the night, before only to train some more. Here's the reality of it all: it will pay off at some point.

You are going to win major victories in your life, and you will lose some too; but know that with every loss you have the responsibility to start again. Don't quit just because you miss the mark. Instead, reach further next time. Remember when Peter walked on the water with Jesus (Matthew 14:22-33)? The Bible says he began to ***sink***. Ordinarily, wouldn't you fall through water? When Jesus is with you, you might fall or begin to sink, but He takes you by the hand and gently pulls you out. After that, Jesus and Peter walked to the boat together. Peter was back on top of the water! You might fall, but stick with Jesus and you will always be safe.

Proverbs 24:16: For a righteous man may fall seven times and rise again, but the wicked shall fall by calamity.

Prayer:

Lord, open my eyes that I can keep my focus on you. And when I falter, help me not to drown but make it to your destined place safely. Amen.

1. List three good habits do you need to implement in your life?

    1. _____
    2. _____
    3. _____

2. List three bad habits to you need to remove from your life?

    1. _____
    2. _____
    3. _____

3. Now, name two action steps you will take to move in the right direction.

    1. _____
    2. _____

Day Five:

It's in my mind.

There was a pastor from the southern United States who had a mental breakdown. He had been under so much pressure in his life that in one moment, he embraced a way out. He started hearing voices and seeing apparitions. He became so irrational that he had to be hospitalized. Yet in the midst of "checking out," God spoke to his heart and told him how to conquer his trial. "It has to be Spirit over mind," God spoke to this pastor.

Sometimes we rely too much on what we know, how we feel, and what we've seen. The Grace journey that all of us are on requires that we trust God even we aren't able to understand what He is doing in our lives. Putting too much confidence in our own thoughts and abilities is very dangerous, because we are so limited in our ability to be objective.

However, the truth principle lies in the fact that if we submit our thoughts, ideas, and desires to

God, He promised to shape us to think and feel like Him. You don't have to go through life with lots of fear and uncertainty in your mind. God wants to renew your mind daily. When we place the Spirit of God over our mind, we bring order to a sometimes chaotic experience. You can sleep tonight and stop your mind from racing. You have permission to give worry the funeral it needs to be buried. Fear and doubt must be evicted. It starts in your mind, and it can end there too, with God's help.

Romans 12:2-3: "And do not be conformed to this world, but be transformed by the renewing of your mind, that you may prove what is that good and acceptable and perfect will of God. For I say, through the grace given to me, to everyone who is among you, not to think of himself more highly than he ought to think, but to think soberly, as God has dealt to each one a measure of faith."

Prayer:

Spirit of God, like never before, I am in need of your daily renewing. Mold my mind like the clay in the potter's hands that my thoughts and desires will be in line with yours. This is my prayer in Jesus' name.

Questions:

1. Identify your biggest "mental" struggle.

   _____
   _____

2. What does "renew your mind" mean to you?

   _____
   _____

3. List three things that contribute to stress in your life and cause you to feel like you are having a breakdown. Why do you think people experience mental breakdowns? Have you ever had or been close to having one? Make a list of things you can do for yourself to prevent a meltdown.

   1. _____
   2. _____
   3. _____

Day Six:

Why do I need this? (the past)

Everything that you have experienced in life is playing a part in how you think and ultimately handle what comes to your life. It's important for you to identify the major moments in your past that are shaping where you are and where you are going.

Why do you need to find your way to grace? Because you have a past. Somewhere along the journey, up until this very moment, you messed up. You spoke out of turn, prejudged someone before meeting them, or maybe you even disobeyed a command from the Lord. Whatever it might be, God wants to give you grace. Grace doesn't take away the things that have happened; rather, grace allows us a license to move forward.

Grace is important, because without it you will constantly rehearse the details of the missteps that mark your past. So you did it. Yes, it is terrible that it happened. Now, let's go forward. Your value to the world diminishes when you are held up from growing into the person God predestined you to be. Acknowledge your past and find strength for your present and future. The world is waiting on you.

2 Corinthians 12: 9-10: "And He said to me, 'My grace is sufficient for you, for My strength is made perfect in weakness.' Therefore most gladly I will rather boast in my infirmities, that the power of Christ may rest upon me. Therefore I take pleasure in infirmities, in reproaches, in needs, in persecutions, in distresses, for Christ's sake. For when I am weak, then I am strong."

Prayer:

Lord Jesus, allow my heart to live in the freedom of your grace. I no longer want my past to haunt my present and future. I acknowledge the things that have happened, but I am ready to move to a better day. My eyes are on you. In Jesus' name, amen.

Questions:

1. Create a list with 3 of the biggest mistakes you feel you have made.
   1. _____
   2. _____
   3. _____

2. Take a moment and pray for grace and freedom from the item you listed on your "worst" list.

3. Read 2 Corinthians 12 in its entirety.

Day Seven:

Why I need this (the present)

Remember the feeling of standing at the edge of the swimming pool? Standing there trying to muster up the courage to jump and plunge into a place where you know your survival is limited? Yet, you long to be cooled off and venturing into the unknown. "Should I or shouldn't I? Should I or shouldn't I?" you keep rehearsing in your mind until a force within you yells, "Go!" and you jump.

In that moment, faith came alive in you. Fear was overcome. In that moment you had everything you needed to simply be happy. What if I told you that, that moment, that feeling, is exactly what Grace wants to be in your life? You are no longer a slave to your past, but you are enjoying your present. In the place you are right now in life, are you happy in it? This is a NOW MOMENT. You have a responsibility to yourself to be active in creating a space to be happy and whole. Lazy thoughts must leave; slothful movements have to cease. This is your finest hour yet!

The Apostle Paul writes in Philippians 4:11-13, "I am not saying this because I am in need, for I have learned to be content whatever the circumstances. I know what it is to be in need, and I know what it is to have plenty. I have learned the secret of being content in any and every situation, whether well fed or hungry, whether living in plenty or in want. I can do all this through him who gives me strength."

Everything may not be perfect, but it can be good. Grace is again giving you permission to be okay, because God is giving you strength. You need this, because you have to live in the present. You have to be present in your thoughts, present with your family, present on your job—there is no more hiding in who you used to be or what you're not. Grace is alive in you, and now you know it.

Philippians 3:13b-14: "But one thing I do: Forgetting what is behind and straining toward what is ahead, I press on toward the goal to win the prize for which God has called me heavenward in Christ Jesus."

Prayer:

God, I want to live in the PRESENT! I am so sick of reliving the past. Guide me, oh thou great Savior, to live in my NOW moment. I am pressing on to what's before me. In Jesus' name, amen.

1. List three things that are going well in your life right now. List three things that you feel could be better.

    1. _____
    2. _____
    3. _____

2. What do you feel God wants you to focus on today? What is in your NOW moment that you need to be focused more on?

    _____
    _____
    _____
    _____

Day Eight:
Why I need this (the future)

Jim was excited to celebrate his fiftieth birthday simply because his wife told him that she had something planned. He didn't know what it was, the location, or the time. All he had was a promise that something was planned. Brenda blindfolded Jim and told him to trust her. She held his hand and led him to the car. He could tell it wasn't their family car, and anticipation only built inside of Jim as he felt every bump and turn of the mysterious vehicle until finally it stopped. Still unaware of what was coming next but living moment to moment off of the promise of his wife, Jim and Brenda walked hand in hand into the silent building.

"Honey, remove your blindfold," Brenda told Jim.

"Surprise!" A chorus of people spontaneously burst into the Stevie Wonder MLK Birthday song. Jim was so surprised and overwhelmed yet satisfied to see all of his family and friends. Before he greeted the guests, he turned and hugged his wife.

Just like Brenda did with Jim, God has made it clear that He has a plan for your life and He wants to take you there. Many times we aren't willing to be like Jim and just go on a promise. Grace is a mechanism that allows us to follow God wherever He is taking us even though it's scary. You need access to this grace to go forward. Grace says, "Just stay with me. I have a plan." Intellect, intuition, and the senses are not your greatest ally. Faith is. Stay with God, and He will bring you into a surprise you never could have imagined.

Jeremiah 29:11-14a: "For I know the plans I have for you," declares the Lord, "plans to prosper you and not to harm you, plans to give you hope and a future. Then you will call on me and come and pray to me, and I will listen to you. You will seek me and find me when you seek me with all your heart. I will be found by you," declares the Lord.

Prayer:

Lord, I don't know exactly what you have in store for me, but I want it all. I pray that I trust you more than ever because you have leading me to a future and a hope. I just want to keep following. Holy Spirit, I need your help. In Jesus' name, amen.

Questions:

1. What does the word "hope" mean to you? What are you hoping for?

   _____

2. How can you commit to "sticking" with God more? What will you do if your answer takes longer than you feel like it should?

   _____
   _____
   _____
   _____

3. Decide three faith moves you will make in this phase of your growth. Write down two things that challenge your faith to grow and get stronger.

   1. _____
   2. _____
   3. _____

Day Nine:

My hunger exceeds my reach

It's 11:59 a.m. and your stomach growls. You can feel the knots churning because lunch time is almost here, but you can't figure out what to eat. All you know is that you're really hungry. "Let's go to the buffet around the corner," your coworker says, and you readily agree because unlimited food seems like the answer to your hunger issue.

So there you are, in the restaurant, with a plethora of choices, so hungry it feels like your stomach has started to eat itself. But here's the problem: you can't figure out what to eat. You are hungry but confused. Starving and yet unsure. In the right place but overwhelmed by the options.

When we arrive at the "Grace Place," its role is to fill the emptiness that has been growing inside of you. Sometimes grace feels like a free ride to do whatever you want, but grace is less concerned about the options and more concerned with you making the right choices through your

God consciousness. One of the most difficult realities of grace is not getting caught up in the availability of options but just focusing on honing in to God's voice. The scriptures reveal the sound of God's voice so that you can hear it in everyone and everything and know for sure it's God. I know you're spiritually hungry, but God will use His grace to help you separate what you want from what you need.

Deuteronomy 28:1-6: If you fully obey the Lord your God and carefully follow all his commands I give you today, the Lord your God will set you high above all the nations on earth. All these blessings will come on you and accompany you if you obey the Lord your God: You will be blessed in the city and blessed in the country. The fruit of your womb will be blessed, and the crops of your land and the young of your livestock—the calves of your herds and the lambs of your flocks. Your basket and your kneading trough will be blessed. You will be blessed when you come in and blessed when you go out."

Prayer:

Lord, I need focus. Help me sharpen my spiritual eyes to see what you want me to discover. I no longer want to get caught up in the options but desire to be spot on in seeing what's right for my life. Only you can help me achieve this. I am walking with you, in Jesus' name, amen.

Questions:

1. List two examples of times when you didn't obey God. Consider: were the outcomes favorable?

    1. _____

    2. _____

2. What do you think it will take for you to be more obedient to God? Express your commitment to following God's instruction by writing down a statement of commitment.

    _____
    _____
    _____
    _____

Day Ten:

Grace: A Gift Others Need

To survive in a place of grace, you first have to give it to others. This can be at times one of the most difficult things to do. Asking for forgiveness takes a lot of self-awareness; it requires being vulnerable, honest, and willing to face the fear of being wrong. On the contrary, to bestow the unbelievable gift of grace simply requires denial of self. Not that getting over your emotions, frustration, and other feelings is simple, but grace is simple.

As we continue this journey of finding our way to grace, we have considered a lot about ourselves. You considered your history, your present, and your future; but growing in grace, though an inward pursuit, demands that you also consider those around you. In order to receive and live in the "Grace Place," you must be willing to give grace to others without prejudice or compensation.

Giving grace to others has nothing to do with what they've done or where they've been. It has everything to do with who they are becoming. This will take practice—much practice. God is asking us to give to others what we need. When you mess up, you simply don't need someone going on and on about what you did wrong, reminding you over and over of the mistake you made. You're well aware of your mishap. You need someone to constantly remind you that though you made a mistake, you can get better. You can learn from the error and become an even better you. Grace is that reminder. When we give grace to others, we liberate them from the bondage of fear and shame and give them a hand up to the place God is growing them to.

Luke 6:37-38: "Do not judge, and you will not be judged. Do not condemn, and you will not be condemned. Forgive, and you will be forgiven. Give, and it will be given to you. A good measure, pressed down, shaken together and running over, will be poured into your lap. For with the measure you use, it will be measured to you."

Prayer:

Father, in the name of Jesus, I know I need help giving grace to others. Take out the stony heart and put in the heart of flesh. Help me see myself in the struggles of others. Remove pride and haughtiness from my heart. In your holy and precious name I pray, amen.

1. Name three people closest to you that you need to give more grace?

    1. _____
    2. _____
    3. _____

2. What steps can you take to operate in grace first and emotions second?

    _____
    _____
    _____
    _____

Day Eleven:

Grace: A gift I need

There is no greater expression of grace than when we look to our Savior as He is hanging on the cross. He is ridiculed, hated, and debated, and yet He doesn't look to repay others for the horrible crimes they've committed against Him. Instead, He prays for them, looks out for them, and still blesses them.

It is important that we see ourselves as the people around the cross on that day. We serve a holy and righteous King who has given us decrees of His expectation for how we should live. We don't always live up to His expectation for our lives. Our sins are like the mockers and jeerers ridiculing Jesus.

Yet, God knows us better than we know ourselves, and He knows what we need. That's why God has given us grace. You need this gift to no longer be in bondage to what you have been. Once Christ pleaded for you and finished his work at Calvary, God no longer holds the guilt of your sins over your head. You still have responsibility for the sin that is at work in you, but God is freeing you from the shame of what you've done or might do.

Have you shouted yet? Are you dancing? You need this gift to be finally free to be—to be a person who makes mistakes but doesn't live *as* a mistake. Free to love yourself as you are and not judge yourself rotten because you finally realize that God really isn't through with you yet. Grace is so alive in you that you are better, and you're more conscious than you've ever been as you you are being transformed into the image of Christ. Who knew grace was this liberating?

Romans 8:14-15, 29-30: "For those who are led by the Spirit of God are the children of God. The Spirit you received does not make you slaves, so that you live in fear again; rather, the Spirit you received brought about your adoption to sonship. And by him we cry, 'Abba, Father.' For those God foreknew he also predestined to be conformed to the image of his Son, that he might be the firstborn among many brothers and sisters. And those he predestined, he also called; those he called, he also justified; those he justified, he also glorified."

Prayer:

Lord Jesus, thank you for loving me so much that you freely give the gift of grace. I know I need it daily, and you give it. Father, your love is overwhelming, but I don't ever want you to take it away. I am happy to live in your grace. Again Lord, thank you. Amen.

Questions:

1. As you access the grace you've been given by God, write a letter to yourself and say all the things you've ever wanted to say but haven't. Be open and honest with your feelings. Then read the letter back to yourself out loud.

2. What did your letter bring you face-to-face with about yourself?

   _____
   _____
   _____
   _____
   _____
   _____

Day Twelve:
Freedom ain't free

A psalmist penned the words, "Count up all it takes to walk with Jesus. Count up all the cost and with courage press your way. Make up your mind to suffer if you would have Him reign and when the battle is raging, give glory to His name."

Grace is unbelievable. It's amazing and it is free, but it does cost something. If someone tells you they have a free item for you and all you have to do is come and pick it up, the item is totally free, but it cost you the work of coming to get it. There is no charge, but there is an associated cost. Grace is no exception. To walk in and live the grace life, there is a cost. You have to give up being judgmental. You have to give up being scornful. You must relinquish the ever easy "If I were you" in exchange for the heart of God.

The cost of Grace is you must increase your love. The Apostle Paul says in 1 Corinthians

13:7 that love "always protects, always trusts, always hopes, always perseveres." The cost of this freedom that Grace gives is that it always seeks to cover instead of expose. We live in a time where people are always quick to expose the weaknesses of others, but Grace doesn't do that to us. Aren't you glad that every ill or wrong deed that you have thought or done hasn't been exposed? That is only possible because grace is at work in and around you.

John 12:24: "Very truly I tell you, unless a kernel of wheat falls to the ground and dies, it remains only a single seed. But if it dies, it produces many seeds."

Prayer:

Holy Spirit, I need your heart. Help me see the opportunities to show love greater than I have ever shown it. I thank you for the example of love in Christ Jesus. I want to conform to his image more now than I have ever in my life. Help me, Holy Spirit. In Jesus' Name, amen.

1. Write three things about the grace life that is challenging? Does it feel natural?

   1. _____
   2. _____
   3. _____

2. Explain how the word of God challenges the reservations you have about grace?

   _____
   _____
   _____
   _____
   _____
   _____

Day Thirteen:

Setting continuous goals

Here we are! Only one day left to go, and you are embracing grace like a cold, crisp glass of water on a hot summer afternoon. Once you put this book down, you will have a lot of work to do to continue to live in this grace consciousness. It is important that you keep in mind that you are changing and developing and getting even better at being you. Your desires are changing to be more like the Father; your heart for others seeks to love them and not focus on their issues; you can look in the mirror and see yourself truly as not what you should be but thankfully not what you used to be.

Remember, however, that the journey is not over just because this book has ended. You must now practice the grace you've been finding your way toward. You must set goals for yourself. Every day should begin with a regimen that includes a confession of who you are becoming. Your confession should be composed of declarations that are what God says about you. Even if the confession doesn't reflect who you are right now, begin to say it daily, because it will align you with where God is taking you.

Remember that grace already knows who you are, but it's more focused on where you are going. Goal setting holds us accountable for what we know must happen. It's not good enough to say, "I just want to be a good person." What does that mean? Who gets to determine what's good and what's not? We are obedient to God's system because He has a set plan and will that holds us accountable for what we want to accomplish with our lives.

Isaiah 55:10-11: "As the rain and the snow come down from heaven, and do not return to it without watering the earth and making it bud and flourish, so that it yields seed for the sower and bread for the eater, so is my word that goes out from my mouth: It will not return to me empty, but will accomplish what I desire and achieve the purpose for which I sent it."

Prayer:

Father, I am asking that you lead me to the things I should be focused on right now. I must minimize the distractions around me and keep my attention on what's truly important. You have sent your word to me. Now let it accomplish what it needs to in my life. In Jesus name, amen.

Questions:

1. Set some goals! Identify three people whom you want to show more grace to. List the things they do that challenge your resolve and plan how you can employ grace to love them better.

    1. _____

    2. _____

    3. _____

2. Write your daily confession and post it somewhere so you can remember to recite it daily.

    _____
    _____
    _____
    _____
    _____
    _____

Day Fourteen:

I'm moving forward, but I'm still me

"I am so going to miss you," George told his son Shane as he prepared to leave him at the dormitory. "You can call home whenever you need to. Don't hesitate. I don't care what time it is. Your mother and I always need to know you're okay."

Shane nodded his head as he hugged his father. George turned and walked out the door, leaving Shane to use for himself every bit of training that he had been given by his father and mother. George knew that he couldn't be with Shane 24/7; he had to trust his son to figure things out on his own.

As you enter the open waters of living the Grace life on your own, God trusts you with the precious treasure of His word, and you've got to work with everything you've learned. The great consolation is that you can call home—on God —whenever you need too. You will find many days will come when you don't feel like being grace filled, but you will learn to call on the Lord, for He promises to answer whenever we call. Though very conscious of the grace active around you, you are still very much yourself with all the idiosyncrasies, proclivities, and desires that you had at the start of this journey. The only difference is that you're accepting the grace to be more than that. You are moving forward.

Take a moment and just think about what it was like before you embraced grace—challenging without a way out, hopeless without a strategy, frustrating without release. But Grace, in all of its wonder, has freed you. Now go: live, dance, love, give, and BE; for you have finally found your way to GRACE. Enjoy.

Hebrews 4:15-16: "For we do not have a high priest who is unable to empathize with our weaknesses, but we have one who has been tempted in every way, just as we are—yet he did not sin. Let us then approach God's throne of grace with confidence, so that we may receive mercy and find grace to help us in our time of need."

Prayer:

Lord, thank you for leading me on this journey to a new life in your Spirit. I embrace grace full and free to bring me to the place you want me to be. I love you and am happy to grow more and more like you every day. This is my sincere prayer, in Jesus' precious and mighty name, amen.

Questions:

1. Name three major realizations this book has provided for you.

    1. _____
    2. _____
    3. _____

2. Know that You can live the Grace life. Grace isn't concerned with the facts of where you are now, it only wants to take you there. Now GO!

For the rest of your life you will be in process: something in your life will always be in development. The Grace life is a process and while it's freely given by God without measure, the extent of how much you receive depends on how aware you are of its presence.

And the God of all grace, who called you to his eternal glory in Christ, after you have suffered a little while, will himself restore you and make you strong, firm and steadfast. To him be the power for ever and ever. Amen.

(1 Peter 5:10-11 NIV)

www.ingramcontent.com/pod-product-compliance
Lightning Source LLC
Chambersburg PA
CBHW040209020526
44112CB00039B/2850